THE PLAIN-ENGLISH GUIDE TO ECONOMIC SANCTIONS FOR INSURANCE COMPANIES

By Heidi Hunter

Lil Abby Press

St. Paul, Minnesota

The Plain-English Guide to Economic Sanctions for Insurance Companies

Copyright © 2024 Heidi Hunter

First Edition: October 2024

Published by LilAbby Press
St. Paul, Minnesota

ISBN: 979-8-9907044-6-6 (e-book)
ISBN: 979-8-9907044-7-3 (paperback)

cover design by Heidi Hunter

Table of Contents

Disclaimer

The information provided in this book is for informational purposes only and is not intended to constitute legal advice. The author of this book is not an attorney, is not providing legal advice, and is not creating an attorney-client relationship with the reader.

Readers should not act or rely on any information in this book without seeking the advice of a lawyer. Any reliance upon the information contained in this guide is solely at the reader's own risk.

The author makes no representations or warranties about the completeness, accuracy, reliability, or suitability of the information in this book.

While every effort has been made to provide accurate and complete guidance, it's critical to understand that this guide does not guarantee an effective sanctions compliance program free from fines or penalties. Compliance with economic sanctions regulations is a complex and evolving area, and the effectiveness of any program depends on various factors, including the specific circumstances of the reader's business and the actions of relevant regulatory authorities. Therefore, the author cannot guarantee specific outcomes or results from implementing the suggestions provided in this guide. This information is a tool to develop and enhance your sanctions compliance program, but the ultimate responsibility for compliance rests with the reader and their organization.

In no event shall the author be liable for any loss or damage whatsoever arising from, or in connection with, the use of the information contained in this book.

Introduction

Economic sanctions are powerful tools governments and international bodies use to influence the behavior of nations, organizations, and individuals. Navigating the complex sanctions landscape can be challenging for insurance companies of all sizes. Understanding and managing the risks associated with sanctions is crucial to ensure compliance and avoid severe penalties. Civil and criminal penalties can exceed several million dollars and lead to negative publicity about your company, damaging your reputation with customers and business partners.

Sanctions compliance isn't just about avoiding fines, though. It is also about upholding ethical and legal standards while navigating a complex global landscape and protecting your company's reputation in the marketplace.

Welcome to *The Plain-English Guide to Economic Sanctions for Insurance Companies.* This guide discusses sanctions issues unique to commercial and consumer insurance companies. It's designed to clearly explain economic sanctions, how they affect the insurance industry, and what steps organizations can take to stay compliant.

Whether you're a sanctions professional dealing with these issues every day, a new employee in the field, or someone who doesn't work directly with sanctions but needs to grasp the key concepts, this guide will provide valuable insights to help you navigate the complexities of sanctions compliance.

If you're new to sanctions or want a refresher, the first book in this series, *The Plain-English Guide to Economic Sanctions,* provides a good overview. This guide assumes you are at least familiar with the concepts and terms in that guide. For more detailed information on how to implement some concepts in this guide, such as your economic sanctions program or risk assessment, my previous guides, *The Plain-English Guide to Economic Sanctions Risk Assessments* and *The Plain-English Guide to Developing an Economic Sanctions Program,* can assist you further.

This guide will mainly focus on economic sanctions enforced by the Office of Foreign Assets Control (OFAC). We'll also briefly touch on other types of sanctions managed by agencies like the Department of State and the Bureau of Industry and Security. Since the insurance industry operates globally, we'll also cover compliance with foreign sanctions regulations.

Throughout the guide, you'll find examples of OFAC fines related to various activities. In my previous role, people often asked if other insurance companies had faced consequences for the actions I was trying to prevent. These examples will help you explain the risks to your company for engaging in activities that may violate sanctions.

Definitions

Some of the terms referenced in this guide are defined below.

Additional Insureds

Someone other than the policyholder covered under the policy. This can include branches, subsidiaries, employees or directors, or counterparties with an interest in the policy.

Beneficiary

The person or entity legally designated to receive the benefits of a financial product such as life insurance.

Beneficial Owner

The person who ultimately owns, benefits, or controls an asset.

Bordereau

A report sent by an insurance company to its reinsurer listing policies covered or claims paid under the reinsurance contract. There are premium bordereaux and claims bordereaux.

Business Partner

Any third party you do business with. A business partner can be a vendor, a subcontractor, an attorney, a joint venture partner, a consultant, or an agent and representative acting on a company's behalf.

Claimant

The person or entity that requests payment from an insurance company for a loss covered by a policy. The claimant could be the named insured, or it could be a third party seeking compensation.

Comprehensive Sanctions

A trade embargo against a country. Most transactions are prohibited.

Economic Sanctions

The government's restrictions or penalties on individuals, entities, groups, governments, or countries to achieve particular foreign policy or national security goals.

Environmental Scan

Environmental scanning is how you, as the sanctions compliance professional, stay updated on changes in economic sanctions regulations.

Facilitation

Assisting others in conducting a transaction that violates sanctions if you had conducted it yourself.

Freezing or Blocking Assets

Preventing a sanctioned party from accessing or using assets you hold that belong to them, such as a bank account or an insurance policy. Assets are deposited into a blocked bank account when possible.

Indirect

Selling goods or services to someone acting on behalf of a sanctioned party or country.

Internal Controls

Internal controls are the processes, procedures, and measures that prevent and detect sanctions violations.

List-Based Sanctions

Programs where sanctioned parties are added to the Specially Designated Nationals (SDN) list. Most transactions with them are prohibited, and assets you hold that belong to them may need to be blocked.

Lloyd's Syndicate

The Lloyd's Syndicate in the UK allows multiple insurance companies to share risks for large or high-risk policies. Insurers can be the lead on a policy or on a tier or follow the lead of another insurer on a tier.

Nexus

Transactions connected to the US, such as participation by a US party, sale of a US good or service, and transacting in US dollars or through the US financial system. The term is also used when referencing whether a particular transaction, claim, or policy has a connection to a sanctioned country, party, or good.

OFAC Sanctions

Sanctions administered by the Office of Foreign Assets Control (OFAC). You'll see terms like "economic sanctions," "OFAC sanctions," "trade sanctions," "sanctions regulations," "OFAC regulations," and "US sanctions" used interchangeably in this guide.

Policyholder

The individual or entity who purchases and owns the policy. They are listed as the primary insured in a policy.

Possible Match/False Positive/Positive Match

A possible match occurs when your sanctions screening system determines your customer may be a match to a person on the SDN list. A possible or potential match is also known as an "alert" or a "hit." A positive match, on the other hand, is a possible match that is determined to be an actual match once your customer's information is compared to the sanctioned party's information.

Risk Assessment

A risk assessment is a method for identifying, analyzing, and addressing a company's sanctions risks. It helps pinpoint any weaknesses in the program and lays out a plan to fix them.

Sanctioned Party

An individual, company, organization, group, government, vessel, or aircraft sanctioned by OFAC and listed on the Specially Designated Nationals (SDN) list.

Sanctions Compliance Officer (SCO)

The person within an organization with ultimate responsibility for the sanctions compliance program.

Sanctions Compliance Program (SCP)

The policies, procedures, and controls that help a company comply with sanctions regulations.

Sanctions Compliance/Sanctions Compliance Team

Sanctions compliance is the function within a company responsible for managing the policy, program, and controls related to sanctions compliance. The SCO is part of this function. This function may also include a separate team dedicated to sanctions (i.e., the Sanctions Compliance Team).

Sanctions Program

A sanctions program consists of all the laws, Executive Orders, OFAC regulations, guidance, licenses, and FAQs related to restrictions against a specific country or activity. It governs what you can and cannot do.

Sanctions Evasion

Sanctions evasion occurs when people try to structure a transaction to get around sanctions.

Sectoral Sanctions

Sectoral sanctions prohibit certain activities in targeted industries with designated entities, while any other activity is legal.

Sanctions Risk

Sanctions risk refers to potential threats or weaknesses that, if not adequately managed by internal controls, can result in violations of OFAC's regulations.

Scanning/Screening

Reviewing a customer or transaction to see if there is a potential sanctions issue. This can involve scanning a name against OFAC's watchlists or reviewing a transaction for a sanctions nexus.

The 50 Percent Rule

Entities majority-owned (50 percent or more) by one or more blocked persons, either through direct or indirect ownership, are also considered sanctioned despite not being named on a watchlist.

US Person

US citizens anywhere in the world, US-incorporated businesses, including their foreign branches, people who are in the US for any reason, even if they are citizens of another country, and any persons transacting in the US financial system, US dollars, or US goods.

Watchlists

Watchlists are lists maintained by OFAC of sanctioned parties. These lists can be Specially Designated Nationals (SDN) lists and non-SDN lists. These lists specify various prohibitions, from full asset and transaction bans (for those on the SDN lists) to targeted restrictions (for those on the non-SDN lists).

Writing Company

The insurance entity that issues a policy. The name of the writing company will appear on the policy. Larger insurance companies may have multiple writing companies depending on the product and state or foreign jurisdiction where the policy is written.

1
Brief Introduction to Sanctions

This chapter briefly summarizes concepts discussed in the first guide, *The Plain-English Guide to Economic Sanctions*. This guide assumes you are at least familiar with the concepts and terms in that guide.

Governmental Agency Responsible for Sanctions

The Office of Foreign Assets Control (OFAC), part of the US Department of the Treasury, oversees most US sanctions programs. OFAC enforces US sanctions laws civilly, while the Department of Justice handles criminal violations of these laws.

Some trade sanctions are managed by different agencies like the Department of State (DoS) and the Bureau of Industry and Security (BIS) of the Department of Commerce. These export control restrictions work alongside OFAC sanctions. They are important for insurance companies providing Ocean Marine insurance, product liability, or other coverage involving exportable goods. You shouldn't provide insurance coverage for transactions violating DoS or BIS restrictions.

Sanctions Programs

Sanctions programs are administered by OFAC and consist of all the laws, Executive Orders, OFAC regulations, guidance, licenses, and FAQs related to restrictions against a specific country or activity. Some programs target activities in certain countries, while some target specific activities globally, such as narcotics trafficking and weapons proliferation.

A country program does not mean that only people in that country are sanctioned. Parties anywhere in the world can be sanctioned under any program.

Also, programs may not exist indefinitely. For example, Sudan used to have a comprehensive sanctions program, but it was discontinued several years ago, and Sudan is currently subject to only minimal sanctions.

The best place to find all of these documents is under the specific program's page on the OFAC website, the link for which is provided under References.

Other Countries That Use Sanctions

Many countries have their own sanctions rules. Some examples include the US, UK, Canada, Japan, and Australia. Even the European Union, comprised of many countries, has its own sanctions regime. Countries that are part of the EU have to follow the sanctions set by the EU,[1] but they can also add more prohibitions of their own.

Types of Economic Sanctions

The term "sanctions" covers a wide range of actions the United States can take against a country, government, person, group, or industry, depending on what activity the US wants to stop. Generally, sanctions fall into three categories: list-based, comprehensive, and trade sanctions.[2]

Comprehensive

Comprehensive sanctions, or trade embargoes, apply to a whole country. They restrict almost all commercial and financial activities involving the sanctioned country, including its government, individuals, businesses, and anyone acting on behalf of that country.[3]

Countries like Cuba, Iran, Syria, North Korea, and specific areas of Ukraine under Russian control, such as Crimea, face comprehensive sanctions from the US. However, current sanctions against Russia are nearly as comprehensive.

List-Based

When a party is sanctioned under one of OFAC's programs, they are added to a watchlist that determines what business, if any, you can do with them. A wide range of parties can end up on the SDN list, including individuals, companies, groups, ships, aircraft, and even cryptocurrency wallets. Parties can appear on more than one type of list.

Parties on the **Specially Designated Nationals (SDN) Lists** will face penalties like asset freezes, travel limits, import/export restrictions, and financial bans.[4] You also cannot do business with them.

Parties on **Non-SDN Lists** are not SDNs and are not subject to blanket prohibitions. Instead, they are subject to specific penalties, including export controls, import bans, financial transaction restrictions, and sectoral sanctions.

There are several non-SDN lists with different purposes, including:[5]

- *Sectoral Sanctions Identifications (SSI) List* - This list focuses on certain sectors of the economy and specific parties operating in those sectors. It is used primarily in the Ukraine-/Russia-related Sanctions program.[6] Even though the SSI restricts certain activities by targeted parties (such as debt/equity restrictions), other dealings with these entities are still allowed, and their assets aren't frozen.

- *Non-SDN Menu-Based Sanctions List (NS-MBS List)* - Parties on this list are not SDNs and are not covered by full blocking sanctions. Each party on the list can have different prohibitions. Their assets aren't blocked, but they face trade or financial restrictions, like restrictions on providing certain goods or services and prohibitions on importing goods.[7]
- *Non-SDN Chinese Military-Industrial Complex Companies List (NS-CMIC List)* - These are Chinese companies that OFAC has determined have Chinese military ties. Again, they are not subject to full blocking sanctions. Instead, OFAC prohibits investment in these companies (i.e., purchasing their debt or equity such as stocks, bonds, or the mutual funds that invest in them).

Sectoral or Trade Sanctions

Sectoral or trade sanctions are the most complicated category to comply with. They prohibit specific activity with targeted entities in specified industries, while any other activity is legal. They can also bar some goods from being exported to or imported from the sanctioned country. The purpose is to weaken the country economically by targeting its most significant industries, pushing it to end its unwanted behavior.

By definition, comprehensively sanctioned countries have trade sanctions. Let's discuss other types of trade sanctions and how they are used, using Russia as an example.

Targeting Industries

Russian industries affected by sectoral sanctions include energy, financial, and minerals and mining, among others. Entities operating in these sectors in Russia can be hit with either blocking sanctions or non-SDN prohibitions.

Targeting Services

US persons are prohibited from providing certain services to parties in Russia, such as quantum computing, architecture, engineering, accounting, trust and corporate formation, and management consulting services.[8] US persons who do business in these sectors in Russia can be sanctioned. However, the restrictions do not prohibit US persons from providing other services not covered by these sanctions.[9]

Targeting Import/Exports

Trade sanctions can prohibit the import of certain Russian goods into the US, such as fish and seafood, alcohol, and diamonds;[10] oil and petroleum products;[11] and Russian-origin aluminum, copper, and nickel,[12] among other items.

In coordination with OFAC, BIS and DoS have imposed export restrictions on numerous US-origin goods that cannot be exported to Russia. These items include electronics, mechanical components, technical components, manufacturing equipment, machine tools, and parts that can be used in Russia's military systems.[13]

Again, sectoral and trade sanctions don't mean that a US person can't conduct any transactions with targeted companies as long as the business does not include the sanctioned activity or goods.

Sanctioned Parties Not on Any List

The most challenging part of complying with sanctions is when parties are considered sanctioned despite not appearing on any SDN or Non-SDN list. This can occur in a couple of ways.

First, some OFAC sanctions block categories of persons even if they do not appear on the SDN List.[14] For example, for the Venezuelan sanctions program, Executive Order 13884 blocks any person who meets the definition of the "Government of Venezuela."[15] Also, OFAC's Cuba sanctions prohibit most transactions with Cuban nationals.[16]

The second way is commonly referred to as the "50 Percent Rule."[17] This rule kicks in when a company is majority-owned (50 percent or more) by one or more sanctioned parties. This includes both direct and indirect ownership. These entities are considered sanctioned even if they aren't on the SDN list.

There is no official government list of companies owned by sanctioned parties, but some private companies, like Dow Jones, create and maintain such lists.

Let's look at an example of how this works. Goode Company has three owners: Bad Co., which is on the SDN list, owns 30 percent of the company; Worst Inc., which is also on the SDN list, owns 25 percent of the company; Best LLC, which is not on the SDN list, owns the remaining 45 percent. Because two of the owners of Goode Company are SDNs, and together they own 55 percent of the company (a majority), Good Company is also considered an SDN, even though they are not on the SDN list.

Note that Best LLC is not sanctioned, despite being an owner of Goode Company and a partner with Bad Co. and Worst Inc. Just because a branch or subsidiary is sanctioned does not automatically make a parent company sanctioned.

2
Who Must Comply with Economic Sanctions?

Who has to comply with economic sanctions? Everyone, including you and your organization! OFAC's definition of who must comply with US sanctions is broad and can include persons or entities not located or operating within the US.

Who Is a Covered US Person?

US sanctions apply to US citizens anywhere in the world, US-incorporated businesses, including their foreign branches, people in the US for any reason, even if they are citizens of another country, and any persons transacting in the US financial system, US dollars, or US goods.[18] Therefore, you are considered a US person if you work for a foreign branch of a US-based insurance company.

For employees of global companies, it is crucial to know if your foreign entities are organized as a branch or subsidiary of a US-based entity. If it is a branch, it must always follow OFAC rules. If it is a subsidiary, it is not subject to OFAC regulations in most instances.

Who Else May Have to Comply?

However, there are situations where foreign parties may need to comply with US sanctions. These are important to know if you work for a foreign insurance company or a foreign subsidiary of a US-based company.

US-Nexus Transactions

If you work for a foreign insurance company or subsidiary that conducts transactions with a US nexus, then your organization is also considered a US person for those transactions.

US-nexus transactions occur when the transaction has a connection to the US. For example, you conduct transactions through a US-based branch or subsidiary, provide US-based coverage, conduct a transaction involving a US person, insure US-origin goods, do business through a US financial institution (such as when receiving premiums or paying claims), or make a payment using US dollars. Foreign parties, including foreign insurance companies, conducting these transactions must comply with OFAC regulations whenever there is a US nexus.

Secondary Sanctions

Some US sanctions go beyond US borders (i.e., have "extraterritorial reach"). These are secondary sanctions.

Secondary sanctions are penalties imposed by one country on individuals, entities, or governments in another country for engaging in activities that violate the first country's sanctions or policies.[19] This means OFAC can require foreign parties, who aren't considered US persons, to follow its sanctions or face getting sanctioned themselves. Usually, the punishment is getting shut out of the US financial system. Iran, North Korea, and Russia are examples of programs with secondary sanctions.

A recent example of secondary sanctions which encompasses foreign insurance companies:

In late 2023, the US issued a new Executive Order 14114 for Russia.[20] It requires foreign financial institutions (FFIs) to comply with certain US sanctions against Russia. Specifically, FFIs can't do transactions for a sanctioned party in sectors of the Russian economy such as technology, defense, aerospace, and manufacturing. Nor can they conduct any transaction or provide any service or good to Russia's military. OFAC's definition of an FFI includes insurance companies. So, a foreign subsidiary of a US-based financial institution, not otherwise subject to OFAC's Russian-related sanctions, would be subject to these regulations as an FFI.

Let's look at the other situation where foreign subsidiaries must comply with OFAC.

Foreign Subsidiaries of US Entities

Foreign subsidiaries do not generally fall under the definition of a US person who must comply with US sanctions because OFAC defines a US person as a business incorporated in the United States and its foreign branches.

However, the Iran and Cuba sanctions programs have expanded the meaning of a US person to include foreign subsidiaries.

- The Cuban regulation defines "persons subject to the jurisdiction of the United States,"[21] which, in short, includes any entity, wherever organized or doing business, owned or controlled by a US person. This includes foreign subsidiaries.

- Iranian regulations prohibit "an entity owned or controlled by a US person, set up outside the US," from dealing with Iran's government or citizens if that activity would be prohibited when conducted by a US person.[22] Again, this definition includes foreign subsidiaries.

If you work for a foreign insurance company, all of these factors can affect whether a particular policy or claim is subject to US sanctions.

3

Introduction to Economic Sanctions for Insurance

At its simplest, economic sanctions mean you are not allowed to do business with certain countries or parties.

Before proceeding with any business transaction, do your homework to identify any potential sanctions issues. This is especially vital for insurance companies, where one policy can have multiple insureds, claimants, counterparties, and covered jurisdictions.

Types of Insurance Affected by Sanctions

"Insurance" encompasses a wide variety of coverages that your organization may provide and may include:

- consumer insurance for home, auto, umbrella, and "toys" (such as boats or snowmobiles)
- group/employee benefits such as life, health, accidental death and dismemberment, long-term disability, and short-term disability
- commercial insurance, including property, commercial auto, general liability, product liability, workers' compensation, professional liability, employer liability, and management liability
- specialized types of insurance such as data breach/ransomware, kidnap and ransom, and flood
- travel insurance
- ocean marine

My prior company offered all of these insurance products, and each product has its own sanctions concerns, which will be covered in a later chapter.

Globality of Sanctioned Parties

You might believe that if you only do business in the United States with US customers, you don't need to worry about following sanctions rules. But that's not true. People and entities worldwide can be SDNs under the various programs. There are parties located in the US who are sanctioned under programs such as the narcotics trafficking program. Just having US-only business won't keep you safe from violating sanctions.

Globality of Insurance

If you work for an insurer with only domestic (US-based) customers, lucky you! Your sanctions job is more manageable but not non-existent because insurance is ultimately global.

For example, your company provides life insurance only to US persons. Likely, that policy will cover the policyholder anywhere in the world. So, if the covered person travels to their homeland of Iran and dies, now, you must comply with OFAC's Iran sanctions.

Two more examples illustrate this globality:

- Your company provides car insurance that covers car travel to Canada or Mexico. Or you provide insurance coverage for rental cars while the US policyholder is overseas. A claim could arise requiring compliance with foreign sanctions regulations.
- Your US-based business customer sells products overseas. Under a product liability policy, you may get a claim from someone in a foreign country, necessitating compliance with that country's sanctions regulations.

Multiple Jurisdictions May Be Involved

If your company offers insurance products providing coverage outside of the US, you will need to follow sanctions regimes in every country where you do business, which can be several jurisdictions for one policy.

An example of how this works:

Your UK subsidiary holds a Directors and Officers policy for a French-based entity doing business in Cuba and Russia.

- The policy is written by your UK subsidiary, so there is a UK nexus.
- The customer is French, so there is an EU and French nexus.
- The customer is doing business in Cuba, giving you a US nexus, as foreign subsidiaries of US parties are considered US persons by OFAC under the Cuba program.
- The customer is doing business in Russia, a high-risk jurisdiction. The policy is subject to US, UK, and EU sanctions programs, each with subtle differences regarding Russia.
- If there is a covered director in another country, such as Japan, you must also comply with those regulations.

Therefore, for one policy written in the UK, you may have to comply with US, UK, EU, Japan, and more sanctions programs, all at the same time!

Sanctions Differ by Jurisdiction

However, be aware that sanctions regimes differ from country to country, so don't fall into the trap of thinking that if a transaction is legal to conduct in one country, it is okay in another.

Here are some examples of how sanctions rules differ by jurisdiction:

- The US is the only major economy that has a sanctions program against Cuba.
- The EU and UK have "blocking statutes,"[23] which means they do not allow any party subject to EU or UK jurisdiction to comply with regulations that conflict with their own. As such, they don't allow parties to comply with OFAC sanctions (such as for Iran and Cuba) when they conflict with the EU's and UK's sanctions programs. This will be discussed in detail in a later chapter.
- The EU and UK have sanctions programs against some countries that the US does not (such as Tunisia and Guinea-Bissau), so if you are also doing business in the EU and UK, you will want to ensure you comply with these sanctions programs, too.
- The EU's and UK's lists of designated parties may differ from the OFAC's SDN list and each other's. You should also check the lists for these jurisdictions if you do business globally.
- In the EU and UK, the 50 Percent Rule is ownership *or control*[24], whereas in the US, it is only ownership. When doing business in the EU or UK with an entity with SDNs in control of the company (minority owners, executives, and board members, typically), be careful they aren't considered to hold majority control over the company. This is very difficult to determine from practical experience, and if you find yourself in this situation, consult with legal counsel. Also, be aware that the UK's 50 percent threshold begins at 50.01 percent ownership ("more than 50 percent") rather than the 50.00 percent ownership of the US and the EU ("50 percent or more").

When Global Policies Aren't Global

Insurers may issue policies that provide worldwide coverage, but in practice the coverage is not that comprehensive because of OFAC's sanctions programs. Depending on your customer, their industry, or the type of insurance you are providing them, you may not be able to provide coverage in certain countries or cover particular situations.

For example, OFAC has generally said that insurance companies can provide global, group life, health, and travel insurance worldwide.[25] But there are restrictions. If someone dies in a sanctioned country, such as Iran, the insurance proceeds can be paid to the beneficiary. But can you pay an entity in Iran for the reparation of a body back to the US? Or can you pay a foreign governmental entity to get documents related to the death? Even permissible global coverages are a bit more complicated to adhere to in practice for sanctions purposes.

Lloyd's Syndicate

Global insurance companies may participate in the Lloyd's Syndicate. Our UK subsidiary worked with the Syndicate. The Syndicate is a system that allows multiple insurance companies to share risks for large or high-risk policies. Insurers can be the lead on a policy, hold a tier position, or follow the lead of another insurer. A single policy can involve twenty or more insurers. The Syndicate writes many policies involving Russia, either by writing coverage in Russia or for parties that do business in Russia.

OFAC compliance while a member of the Lloyd's Syndicate presents its own challenges.

Since insurers in the Syndicate have different jurisdictions and ownership structures, conflicts often arise about whether a policy or claim violates sanctions, particularly US, UK, and EU sanctions. This is further complicated when your Syndicate underwriters claim that other insurers don't see an issue, pressuring you to follow suit.

However, neither you nor your underwriters will know the specific circumstances of each writing company, their US ownership, or how their sanctions compliance teams reached their decisions. You need to do your research, consult legal counsel when needed, document your conclusions, and stand by your decisions if conflicts occur.

For instance, we requested that Iran or Cuba be excluded territories in a policy written through the Syndicate. However, as a follow line, we often couldn't change policy wording, so if we participated, we had to rely on the sanctions exclusion language of the lead insurer. This isn't foolproof, as UK entities can legally write business involving Cuba and Iran, and as a follow line, your company may be expected to pay those claims.

In one case unresolved when I left, a claim involved an entity potentially majority-owned by a sanctioned party. We had evidence to support this and decided not to pay. The customer argued that their ownership was below 50 percent. Some insurers were willing to pay the claim, others were not.

Make the best decisions for your company's situation, and don't feel pressured to do what other insurers do.

4

Other Nuances about Economic Sanctions

You can see by now that sanctions are not straightforward and are open to interpretation. Here are a few key things to know about sanctions that aren't so obvious in the regulations but are critical to ensuring sanctions compliance.

Foreign Branches Versus Foreign Subsidiaries

Foreign branches are always considered US persons under OFAC regulations. Insurance companies often have complex ownership structures, so it's essential to trace ownership up the chain to determine if a foreign branch is ultimately owned by a US person.

Foreign subsidiaries face different sanctions challenges. They are considered US persons for sanctions related to Iran, Cuba, and North Korea, and they might also need to comply with OFAC's secondary sanctions and other situations with a US-nexus. It's crucial to understand these nuances and how they could impact policies written by your subsidiary.

US Territory

US territory isn't just the fifty states and the District of Columbia. It is broadly defined as "United States, its territories and possessions, and all areas under the jurisdiction or authority thereof."[26] For example, American Samoa and Guam are US territories, so they are not considered foreign countries for sanctions. "Areas under the jurisdiction" include places under US control in foreign countries, like military bases and embassies. So, doing business in those areas isn't viewed as occurring on foreign soil. For instance, Guantanamo Bay in Cuba isn't covered by Cuban sanctions because it is technically under US jurisdiction, not Cuba's. We wrote several policies covering US military activities at Guantanamo without needing a specific license.

Indirect

OFAC prohibits the direct and indirect provision of prohibited goods or services. Direct is self-explanatory, but what is indirect?

If a company sells goods or services to someone acting on behalf of a sanctioned party or country, even without knowing it, they are indirectly doing business with that sanctioned party. For example, if a firm sells computer parts to a wholesaler in India, who then sells them to customers in Russia or Cuba—where the firm is not allowed to sell directly—the firm is indirectly supplying prohibited goods. If your insurance company insures that firm's shipments or provides product liability coverage, you could be liable under OFAC rules for indirectly insuring a prohibited transaction. This is why sanctions exclusion clauses are crucial; they can serve as proof that your company was not covering the prohibited transaction.

Reinsurance can also be considered indirect provision of services to the customer via a third party (the primary insurer).

Facilitation

"Facilitation" means helping others break sanctions rules. It could be offering financial help, organizing support, or providing aid that lets sanctioned people, groups, or countries avoid sanctions.[27] You cannot facilitate a transaction that, if you conducted it yourself, would violate OFAC sanctions. OFAC doesn't allow facilitation, and breaking this rule can have severe legal consequences, as it weakens sanctions and supports illegal actions.

Facilitation could be as simple as referring prohibited business to another company not covered by the OFAC regulation. Our organization was concerned that even referring business to our UK subsidiary—when our domestic companies couldn't write those policies—might be considered facilitation, which could violate sanctions rules. OFAC has fined entities for this type of activity. AL Tank in the US violated Iranian sanctions by referring an Iranian business opportunity to their Middle East affiliate, thereby facilitating a transaction that would have been prohibited if performed by the US entity. [28]

Sanctions Evasion

Sanctions evasion happens when people try to hide or structure transactions to get around sanctions, and insurance companies need to stay alert for it. Common evasion tactics include using straw buyers, creating fake companies, transferring assets to non-sanctioned relatives, trading through third countries, hiding the true origin of goods, or setting up new companies in countries not under sanctions.

For instance, say someone's sanctioned under the Lebanon sanctions program, and a company wants to sell them an appliance. The SDN uses a third party to buy it for them. The selling company is aware of the ultimate beneficial owner of the goods and wants insurance for the goods during shipment. If you know or should have known through due diligence that a transaction you are insuring will ultimately benefit a sanctioned person but still insure it, you could get into big trouble with OFAC.

5

How Economic Sanctions Affect Your Company

Economic sanctions affect the entire company, every employee, and every business line, especially for global insurers.

Of course, if you are a sanctions compliance professional, you are affected, but the need to be knowledgeable about and comply with sanctions does not end with you. Employees who perform any number of tasks with a sanctions nexus are also impacted by economic sanctions.

This is not an exhaustive list of jobs that could be required to have sanctions knowledge and procedures in your company:

- claims adjustors
- payment processors (such as a claim, refund, vendor payment, or funds received)
- underwriters
- product development
- legal/compliance
- contracting
- staffing
- sales
- customer service
- reinsurance contractors

Let's look at a few examples of how some of these positions in an insurance company have a sanctions nexus:

1. Accounts Receivable (AR): AR invoices customers and receives payments. If AR invoices Joe Designee but receives a payment from Jane Designee, both Joe and Jane must be scanned against OFAC's lists to ensure they aren't sanctioned parties. AR staff may need to scan names manually before invoicing and after receiving payments unless an automated system handles this. At a minimum, AR staff should have basic sanctions knowledge for when compliance requests additional information or assistance (such as blocking funds).

2. Sales: Sales teams work with brokers to sell insurance products. They must be aware of sanctions regulations and avoid selling products to sanctioned

brokers or selling prohibited coverage in sanctioned countries, especially if they work with foreign brokers.

3. Human Resources (HR): HR should scan all potential hires to ensure they are not sanctioned before onboarding. This includes employees hired through outside staffing firms. HR must ensure that both the staffing firm and the employees they provide are not sanctioned.

4. Claims Adjusting: Claims adjusters review claims and issue payments. All payees must be scanned before payment is made. For payments going to foreign countries, they need to confirm the country is not comprehensively sanctioned and that the payment isn't going to a sanctioned bank. Claims adjusters must understand sanctions well, as claims can also involve prohibited goods or sanctioned locations, which could lead to violations if a claims adjustor doesn't recognize a potential issue and refer it to sanctions compliance for review.

5. Underwriting: Underwriters review insurance applications and decide on coverage. All parties involved in an insurance policy—such as the primary insured, additional insureds, contractors, and counterparties—must be scanned before the policy is issued. Underwriters should also consider other potential sanctions issues, like coverage in sanctioned countries, and know to refer those issues to sanctions compliance for review.

If you think about it, there are few jobs within an insurance company without a sanctions nexus. So it's vital that all employees are trained in sanctions generally and your organization has sanctions procedures for these employees to follow.

6

Insurance Sanctions Compliance Program

Every insurance company needs a strong, written program to identify and resolve insurance-specific sanctions concerns and ensure compliance with sanctions.

A sanctions compliance program (SCP) comprises the policies, procedures, and controls that help a company follow sanctions regulations. Depending on your company's size and whether it operates globally, your program might include some or all of the elements below. This outline is based on real-life experience, industry best practices, and OFAC guidance. [29]

At a minimum, an insurance company should have an SCP that encompasses:

- a Sanctions Compliance Officer (SCO) or other responsible party
- economic sanctions policy
- written procedures
- risk assessment
- training
- internal controls
- contract language
- auditing and testing

More details on each section are below.

Responsible Party

Your program will identify who in the company is responsible for overseeing the program. This could be someone specifically appointed to manage all aspects of the program, provide direct supervision of the sanctions compliance team, and indirectly oversee any additional staff performing sanctions-related duties. This can be a sanctions compliance officer (SCO) or the head of your sanctions compliance team. Alternatively, it could be someone with sufficient authority within the organization, such as the chief compliance officer (CCO) or the chief legal officer (CLO).

Economic Sanctions Policy

A sanctions policy will outline your company's commitment to sanctions compliance and briefly describe the procedures and controls for compliance. The policy should be risk-based, tailored to your company's specific risks, and written in plain, easy-to-read language since everyone in the company will need to be familiar with it. The policy should be reviewed and updated at least annually.

Your policy should include high-level information on the following key components:

- senior management buy-in and commitment to fostering a culture of compliance
- pertinent definitions for key terms such as sanctions, sanctioned parties, prohibited transactions, etc.
- potential penalties to the company and the individual for non-compliance
- who the policy applies to in the company and whether third parties such as vendors and business partners must comply with your policy
- sanctions laws applicable to your company, both domestic and foreign
- who is responsible for administering the policy and for auditing it
- methods to report potential violations

Written Procedures

It's essential to have written sanctions compliance procedures, whether carried out by the sanctions team or employees in other departments. Clear procedures help ensure that everyone follows the rules correctly.

Here are some procedures you might consider for your company. The exact ones you need will depend on your company's risk level, size, and scope of operations:

- how to review and clear alerts from a scanning application
- how and when to manually scan business
- when other departments should refer business to the sanctions compliance team or SCO for review
- how to conduct a risk assessment
- what steps to take if a customer is sanctioned
- how to escalate sanctions issues (such as a potential violation)
- how and when to contact OFAC to file blocked assets and rejected transaction reports, apply for specific licenses, file a voluntary self-disclosure, etc.

Collaborate on procedures with the people responsible for carrying them out. Maintain the procedures in a common area (for example, an online shared site) so the most recent version can be easily accessed.

Procedures should be reviewed and updated at least annually or when there is a significant update to a process.

Risk Assessment

A risk assessment is a method for identifying, analyzing, and addressing a company's sanctions risks. It helps pinpoint any weaknesses in the program and lays out a plan to fix them. Your SCP should be based on risk. A separate written procedure may briefly state how risk is determined and describe in detail how the risk assessment should be conducted. A risk assessment should be updated at least annually.

Training

Everyone in an insurance organization likely needs basic sanctions knowledge and training. Some employees who encounter sanctions issues regularly may require more detailed training. You should describe in your sanctions policy who will receive sanctions training, how often it will be rolled out, how it will be tracked, and who will provide it.

Internal Controls

Internal controls are the processes, procedures, and measures that prevent and detect sanctions violations. Your controls will vary depending on your industry, size, global scope, and the results of your risk assessment. However, these are some of the critical controls you will want to implement:

- scanning/screening of customers and transactions
- customer due diligence
- vendor due diligence
- training
- contract wording
- risk assessment
- auditing and testing
- written procedures
- environmental scanning

Contract Language

An SCP for an insurance company will include the requirement for sanctions exclusion language in policies and third-party contracts. Include the wording you require in your SCP to maintain consistency among policies and products. Sanctions exclusion clauses will be discussed in a subsequent chapter of this guide.

Testing and Auditing

Your sanctions program should be reviewed and tested to identify any gaps in the program that may prevent it from operating effectively. This can be done through periodic compliance testing and auditing. The policy should indicate that testing and auditing will occur, who will conduct it, and the frequency. It's ok to specify the frequency as "periodically" or "at least once every three years."

The second book in this series, *The Plain-English Guide to Developing an Economic Sanctions Program,* goes into more detail about implementing each of these elements.

7
Legal Considerations

One of the most important tools for staying compliant with sanctions is including exclusion clauses in contracts and insurance policies. These clauses state that the contract or policy is void if a sanctions violation occurs, helping you avoid paying for or covering prohibited transactions. You might even have sanctions exclusion clauses in your own personal insurance policies.

OFAC said, "The best and most reliable approach for insuring global risks without violating US sanctions law is to insert in global insurance policies an explicit exclusion for risks that would violate US sanctions law... It essentially shifts the risk of loss for the underlying transaction back to the insured - the person more likely to have direct control over the economic activity giving rise to the contact with a sanctioned country, entity or individual."[30]

We based the sanctions exclusion language in our policies on Lloyd's LMA3100 form[31]. Lloyd's sanctions exclusion language is widely accepted. The language states that the insurer isn't liable for any claim and is not required to provide any coverage under the policy to the extent that it would expose the insurer to sanctions.

This language should be included in all policies, either directly in the contract, as an endorsement, or as a separate notice. How you incorporate the language depends on how easily your forms can be updated and whether those forms must be resubmitted for state review. You may want to use a notice, for example, if revisions to the form would cause a state to reopen and review the entire policy contract language, which could lead to a lot of avoidable work!

When contracting with a vendor for services, ensure the contract mandates compliance with sanctions and that they cannot become sanctioned or payment will not be made under the contract. Consider adding language requiring them to report any sanctions violations to you as part of your ongoing vendor monitoring process.

Sanctions Clauses Are Not Foolproof

Be aware, however, that sanctions clauses may not fully protect you in legal disputes.

The EU and the UK have "blocking statutes."[32] Blocking statutes prevent compliance with foreign regulations, like OFAC sanctions for Iran and Cuba, that conflict with UK or EU laws. This aims to protect UK and EU companies from extraterritorial laws and allow them to conduct business freely.

While the UK and EU governments won't sue US companies for using sanctions clauses, affected companies can bring civil cases against them.

Recent court cases have shown mixed outcomes.

In 2018, the UK High Court ruled insurers aren't liable to pay a claim when payments violate sanctions laws.[33] The Court said the blocking statute did not apply as the sanctions exclusion clause was part of the contract, not a direct response to US sanctions laws.[34]

However, the court also said that payment requirements are only suspended, not eliminated. If sanctions change, the transaction must be completed, possibly causing claims to remain open indefinitely.

In 2019, the UK High Court sided with a defendant who refused payment due to OFAC sanctions. The court stated that the policy clearly outlined sanctions compliance, and the insured should have been aware of the risks.[35]

In 2021, however, the EU Court of Justice ruled that companies under EU jurisdiction can't take action solely to comply with US sanctions if it violates the EU's blocking statute. The company must prove it wasn't seeking to comply with US sanctions laws when it canceled the business but took action for another appropriate reason.[36]

To protect your company from blocking statutes, consider:

- Excluding certain jurisdictions in your contracts. Add territorial exclusion clauses in your contracts to avoid transactions in places like Iran or Cuba alongside sanctions exclusion clauses.
- Relying on other contract clauses. Use general non-compliance with laws and regulations clauses or other legal grounds for ending a contract instead of citing sanctions.
- Applying for a specific OFAC license. You might consider applying for an OFAC license to conduct the transaction. However, you must first get permission (i.e., a license) from the UK or EU authority, and these applications are public. If your customer sees you're trying to comply with US sanctions that conflict with UK or EU sanctions, it might sue you.

So, sanctions clauses can help your company avoid violations of OFAC sanctions and the associated fines, but they may not fully protect against lawsuits under the UK and EU blocking statutes.

8
Identifying Transactions with Sanctions Issues

Insurance companies must be vigilant about complying with sanctions regulations when issuing policies and paying claims. Sanctions violations can occur if policies cover individuals, entities, jurisdictions, or situations subject to restrictions. Here are some example scenarios where completing a transaction would be prohibited:

- An applicant is named on the SDN (Specially Designated Nationals) list.
- The coverage is for property located in sanctioned countries, such as Iran.
- A non-sanctioned party includes a sanctioned bank as an additional insured, like a bank holding a mortgage.
- A non-sanctioned cargo company ships goods, such as oil, to a sanctioned party or country.
- A non-sanctioned individual names a beneficiary who is a sanctioned party.
- A non-sanctioned customer is wholly owned by a sanctioned party.

A number of these situations initially involve non-sanctioned parties. How should an insurance company identify and avoid these situations? The two best ways are implementing a sanctions screening program and a referral process.

Sanctions Screening Program

Most emphasis on complying with sanctions is on scanning, also known as screening. Scanning involves checking a party's name (customer, vendor, employee, payee, etc.) against the OFAC lists to see if there is a match. Surprisingly, OFAC does not require anyone to scan their business. However, no compliance program would be effective without it.

The sanctions screening program should be in writing and consist of the following elements:

- what criteria an automated sanctions screening solution should include
- what sanctions watchlists to include in your scanning program
- what data will be scanned
- how often data will be scanned
- when manual scanning should be conducted
- written procedures for clearing or escalating potential matches
- written procedures for dealing with positive matches

- periodic testing of the application to ensure it's functioning as expected

What Data Should Be Scanned?

Everyone you do business with should be scanned. This includes all customers (including additional insureds and counterparties), beneficiaries, payees (such as claimants), payors who make a payment on an account, employees, vendors, and other business partners such as attorneys or consultants. You should also scan countries you are doing business in to know they are not the target of a trade embargo.

For marine, the list of participants who should be scanned is even longer, including the purchaser, seller, shipper, shipping company, vessel name, consignee, freight forwarder, the ultimate beneficiary of the shipment, countries the shipment is transiting, and goods shipped, among others.

If you insure goods, trade sanctions scanning programs exist that will screen the item to identify if it is prohibited for sale in the jurisdiction where you are providing coverage.

How Do I Scan All These Names?

Most insurance companies should have an automated system through which data from all applications is fed. Some applications that may hold relevant data include claims, vendor management, policy administration, policy application, accounting applications such as Peoplesoft, and payment and reimbursement systems. In addition, in situations where data is not automatically scanned or timely scanned, manual scanning can be conducted. OFAC has a free tool.[37]

Automated Scanning Application

An automated scanning application is the best way to implement a sanctions screening program as, once it's appropriately set up, it should operate with minimal intervention. Some companies that offer sanctions screening systems include Lexis Nexis, Moody's, and Computer Services, Inc. (CSI).

When vetting a system, ask the following questions:

- What watchlists are included? A global insurance company will need lists from countries worldwide, and not all vendors include all of those lists.
- Who keeps the sanctions lists up-to-date? Most vendors will keep the watchlists updated themselves.

- How soon after a list is updated is your system updated? Same-day updating is ideal. OFAC has sanctioned companies for conducting transactions for a party sanctioned on the same day the transaction was made.[38]
- Do they use "fuzzy logic" to identify matches? Fuzzy logic means using variations in spelling, phonetics, and name transposition (switching of first and last names) to determine a potential match. This is a necessary component of a sanctions screening system.
- Can clearing logic be recorded in the system? Clearing logic is the record of how you determined that a potential match is a false positive and not a positive match.
- Can documents be attached in the system? If you use documents to clear an alert, you will want to attach that to the alert for future reference.
- Can you scan data against different watchlists and different thresholds depending on what the data is? Depending on your size and the data you want to scan, you may not want to screen all your data against the same watchlists at the same threshold. For example, if you have international and domestic business, you may want to screen the domestic business only against US lists while screening international business against global lists.
- How long does the system retain the data? Data should be accessible for at least five years in case you need to provide information to OFAC or auditors.
- Is there a whitelist or "good customer list" you can add people to? Once you clear a customer as a match to a sanctioned party, you don't want to look at that alert again.
- Is the system user-friendly?
- Is it easy for your data files to be loaded and scanned through the system?

What Sanctions Lists Should We Use?

OFAC has several watchlists, both SDN lists (full blocking prohibitions) and non-SDN lists (other targeted restrictions). As a US person, you should ensure your scanning system screens them all.

If you have any foreign business, you should include the foreign government sanctions watchlists for the countries where you do business. Some top picks are Canada, the UK, the EU, and Australia. A data set containing all global sanctions watchlists should be utilized if you do business in every country. Dow Jones has such a list that can be fed as a separate watchlist into your screening solution.

What Happens if There Is a Match?

There are a lot of common names on the OFAC lists, so you will likely find a customer who is a name match. This match is usually determined to be a "false positive" (i.e., not an actual match) after comparing your customer information to the information on the SDN provided by OFAC. So, if you scan a name and find a match—don't panic! It is likely not a positive match. Most aren't. Obtaining information from your customer, such as Social Security Number, Date of Birth, or address history, that you can compare to the party on the SDN list should clear this potential match. However, if it is a positive match, the next chapter covers what OFAC expects you to do next.

Remember: What may be okay today may not be tomorrow—programs and watchlists are regularly added or updated—so you need to periodically re-screen all parties.

Referral Process

However, you cannot rely on scanning alone. Your automated system may not identify all sanctions risks for a policy, claim, or vendor.

For example, your customer is US-based, but the coverage includes insuring property in Syria. That information may only appear in the underwriting documents and may not be sent to your screening application.

Or, a claim occurs in Iranian waters, but your screening system only receives data that shows the customer, the claimant, and the vendors involved in the loss are all non-sanctioned.

That is why a referral process is so important!

Our automated system couldn't catch all the sanctions risks in the policies we wrote, so we set up a referral process for underwriters and claims handlers. For higher-risk policies and claims, we created a straightforward procedure for when and how they should refer cases to the sanctions compliance team. We also trained them on this process and explained why it's crucial. Before I retired, we were developing an automated tool to make these referrals more efficient. Employee referrals and automated screening are essential parts of an insurance company's sanctions program.

What transactions should you include in your referral program? Consider any risks linked to comprehensively sanctioned countries or higher-risk nations like Russia and Venezuela or any other high-risk situations identified in your risk assessment. Staff will need a clear understanding of what constitutes a sanctions nexus. For the above two examples, the underwriter would refer the policy as it covers property in Syria, and the claims adjuster would refer the claim as it occurred in Iranian waters.

9

What If My Customer Is Sanctioned?

What you need to do if your customer is sanctioned depends on whether it is a current or prospective customer and whether you have any assets belonging to the customer. It will also depend on what program they are sanctioned under as, again, some sanctions programs only prohibit certain activities, not all.

Stop Doing Business with Them, or Don't Start

For most programs, the first requirement is not doing business with them. This means you cannot open an account, issue a policy, sign a contract to receive goods or services, or process a claim for a party named on the SDN list.

If you already have an open policy or claim or an open contract with a vendor, you must stop working with them immediately. When someone is sanctioned under a blocking program, you can no longer provide any services to them, including activities that would wind down the business, unless a license is issued (discussed in the next chapter). These assets will just sit there until they expire (in the case of a contract or policy) or get frozen (such as funds).

You can apply for a specific license to maintain a policy, such as when a US-based company is owned by a sanctioned parent company. This was the case when Russia's Rusal was sanctioned. Since Rusal America, their US subsidiary, was also considered sanctioned under the 50 Percent Rule, you could apply for a license to keep doing business with them if they were your insurance customer. You also have the option to apply for a license to pay a claim to a non-sanctioned third party.

Freeze or Block Assets

You will see the terms "blocked" or "frozen" used interchangeably, and they mean the same thing: you cannot release those assets to the SDN.[39] Blocking assets for an insurance company is a bit more complicated than for a bank blocking an account.

When a party is sanctioned under a program requiring an asset freeze, you cannot accept payments or assets from them, make payments to them, or provide other economic resources (such as loans from a life insurance policy) to them as of the date they are added to the list.

OFAC expects you to "block" a policy as it's considered an asset, and we did that in my prior position. You are not required to move the policy to a blocked bank account as you would if you held funds, but you will need to work with the line of business to ensure no further activity is performed on the account until the policy expires. If there is a wind-down license, you can try to cancel the policy during the license term if there is sufficient time.

You may also have to block the proceeds of a valid claim owed to an SDN. Again, you can't send the payment, nor can you just deny the claim. If the payment is due to the SDN, it is considered their asset, and you must block it. If the claim is invalid and denied, you don't need to block anything, as there is no asset to block. If you haven't yet reviewed the claim to determine if payment is due, you must pause the process and hold off on further evaluation.

OFAC also does not allow the processing and payment of valid claims for non-sanctioned parties under a frozen policy. The claim, if valid, will need to sit open until such time the payment can be made or a specific license is requested to pay it.[40] This policy differs from the UK and the EU, which allow processing payments to non-sanctioned parties on a claim where the insured is sanctioned, as they don't technically require policies to be "blocked." However, you still cannot pay these claims if there is a US nexus.

If you receive premium payments after the time of the sanction (some customers may try to keep a policy active, thinking the sanction will soon be removed), you will need to block those funds unless there is a wind-down license that allows receiving and returning the funds. Without a wind-down license, you can't return them to the SDN, nor can you apply the payment to their policy.

So, how do you block assets? Generally, funds must be put into a bank account blocked by a bank. The account must be interest-bearing, likely prohibiting your insurance company from maintaining the funds in a separate account internally. Maintaining the funds in an internal account and "imputing" interest (i.e., calculating the amount of interest the SDN would receive if the funds were in a bank account) is also inappropriate.

Once the funds are in this blocked bank account, neither you nor the SDN can access them without permission from OFAC. However, the title to the assets remains with the SDN.[41] It is best to contact OFAC for guidance on blocking assets the first time.

Reject a Transaction

In other programs, rather than freezing assets, there's a prohibition against carrying out a transaction. For example, you may decline to transfer money to a country under comprehensive sanctions, like Iran, where such transactions are banned. However, you wouldn't freeze the assets unless they belong to an SDN. Another instance is when you are sending money for a non-sanctioned customer to a sanctioned bank. Even though the bank is under sanctions, the customer isn't, so the transaction should simply be rejected instead of freezing the assets.

This happened to us occasionally for life insurance claims where the beneficiary resided in a comprehensively sanctioned jurisdiction.

We had beneficiaries in Iran and Syria who were not sanctioned, and the claims were valid. The claim has to be paid within a certain time period if it's a valid claim. So, is another way to legally disburse the funds so the beneficiary can receive them?

For the Iran beneficiary, her daughter in Canada had Power of Attorney. We could legally send her the funds, and she could legally send them to her mother under a personal remittance general license (discussed in the next chapter).

We could not find any way to get the Syrian beneficiary the funds, so they had to be escheated to the state. If the beneficiary ever comes to the US, they could gain access to the funds. You can't distribute the funds to the executor (if they are not a family member) or an attorney acting on behalf of the estate, as they cannot take advantage of the personal remittance general license. Nor can you put the funds in a blocked bank account, as the beneficiary is not an SDN.

Note that beneficiaries in Cuba, whether they are an SDN or not, must have their proceeds put in a blocked bank account first. Then, they can petition to have the funds released to someone in the US who can forward them to Cuba via the personal remittance exception.

Report to OFAC

Any time you block assets or reject a transaction due to sanctions, you must file a report within ten business days of the blocking or rejection.[42] There can occasionally be some confusion about when the ten-day clock starts, but we used when the transaction was completed (e.g., the funds entered the blocked bank account), not when the transaction that needed blocking or rejection was identified.

You can file online at https://ofac.treasury.gov/ofac-reporting-system. Again, it is best to contact OFAC for guidance your first time.

Let's look at an example of how this would work.

Bob's Bullets is a company that sells ammunition. Bob's Bullets becomes an SDN under the weapons proliferation sanctions program for selling ammunition to an entity in Iran. An insurance company will no longer be able to provide insurance to Bob's Bullets, such as workers' compensation or property coverage. Any assets belonging to Bob's Bullets, such as an insurance policy, a pending claims payment, or premium payments received, now must be frozen by the insurance company. Once those assets are deposited into a blocked account, the organization will file a report with OFAC notifying them of the assets being held.

If your company holds blocked assets in a blocked bank account, there is an annual requirement (to be filed by September 30) to report those assets to OFAC. Our bank, which held blocked assets for many different entities, filed the annual report for all its blocked accounts, including ours.

10

Can I Do Any Business with Sanctioned Parties or Countries?

Even though sanctions are in place against certain parties and countries, OFAC does provide ways to legally do business with these parties via a license or non-prohibited transaction.

What Is a License?

A license is permission from OFAC to conduct business normally prohibited by a sanction. There are two types of licenses: general and specific. OFAC established general licenses that can be used by anyone for certain transactions. If no general license is available, you'll need to apply to OFAC for a specific license.[43] A specific license is permission granted by OFAC to a specific party for a particular transaction. Let's take a closer look at these licenses.

General Licenses

OFAC general licenses are available to anyone who believes their activities fit within the terms of the license. You don't need to ask OFAC for permission to use one, and you don't have to tell them you are using it. General licenses can expire, be renewed, or be canceled before they expire.

Some general licenses are called "wind-down licenses." They let you keep doing business with a newly sanctioned party briefly while you wrap up your dealings with them. They do not allow you to continue business as usual.

Some activities are licensed under a general license for several programs, such as those that cover legal services, work of the US government or international organizations such as the Red Cross, telecommunications, internet communications, and protecting intellectual property like patents and trademarks.

Below is a discussion of a couple of the more commonly used general licenses.

Humanitarian Aid

The US generally does not prohibit transactions related to humanitarian aid under its sanctions programs, even for countries with trade embargoes.[44]

OFAC has issued general licenses allowing these transactions in most programs and guidance on complying with them.

So, what is considered humanitarian aid?

Generally, these transactions are linked to agriculture, food, medicine, medical devices, and replacement parts. It can also include activities conducted by nonprofit groups that work toward public and social welfare goals or international organizations that benefit the civilian population by meeting basic human needs or building democracy, such as the United Nations World Food Program.

Since our insurance company insured shipments of food, agricultural supplies, medicine, and medical devices, we had to regularly verify that the shipment fell under this general license.

It is crucial to remember just because someone says a transaction is for humanitarian reasons, don't rely on it. Not everything fits the definition of humanitarian aid in the sanctions regulations. For instance, some pesticides (generally allowed under the agricultural general license) can't be sent to certain countries, like Russia, because they might be used for chemical weapons. Also, some medical devices need a specific license to export.[45] Plus, these humanitarian licenses usually don't let you transfer funds to a sanctioned party. Always ensure the transaction or item is allowed under the humanitarian license for that program.

Personal Remittances

Comprehensive sanctions programs, such as those for Iran, Syria, Cuba, North Korea, and Crimea, permit US individuals to send non-commercial, personal remittances to these countries.[46] General licenses enable financial institutions to process these transactions. With a personal remittance general license, individuals can send money to close relatives in a comprehensively sanctioned area.

However, if the transaction is commercial (e.g., making a purchase or paying an insurance claim), this general license doesn't apply.

For instance, Antonio can send money to his aunt in Cuba without violating US rules. His bank can also process the transfer. But if Antonio were to die and leave his aunt in Cuba the proceeds of his life insurance policy, the payment of the claim to the aunt would be considered a commercial transaction by the insurance company, and the insurer can't use the personal remittance general license to send the funds.

Specific License

A specific license is a written document granted by OFAC to one party for permission to conduct a transaction or series of transactions that would otherwise be prohibited by sanctions.[47] The party who wants a specific license has to apply for it, and OFAC may or may not approve it. Plus, it can take a long time to get one approved. Only parties covered under the specific license can use it.

A customer may request a specific license from OFAC for certain activities (such as shipping certain goods legally to Cuba). However, be sure the customer's license covers all third parties involved in the transaction, including insurance coverage. Otherwise, your organization may need a separate license to insure those transactions. Just because the customer has a license doesn't mean your company does unless you are listed in the license.

In my prior position, we used specific licenses to make payments on claims that would otherwise be prohibited due to sanctions. For example, a maritime incident occurred in Crimean waters, a comprehensively sanctioned jurisdiction. The specific license obtained by the customer allowed the issuance of claims payments and the hiring of third parties to conduct salvage, among other services.

Non-Prohibited Transactions

As mentioned before, depending on the program someone is sanctioned under, you may still be able to do some business with them, just not the activity prohibited under the sanction. This occurs most with parties sanctioned under Non-SDN list programs. If you identify a customer or other party as a positive match, review the program under which they are sanctioned to see what is prohibited.

For example, suppose you want to purchase a product from a company in China. You search the OFAC list and find out they are sanctioned under the Non-SDN Chinese Military-Industrial Complex Companies List. This program prohibits the purchase of public securities of certain Chinese companies due to their ties to the Chinese military. However, it allows other types of transactions, such as purchasing goods.[48] In this example, you can proceed with your transaction, as the prohibitions of this sanctions program do not apply to your purchase.

Our company had a Hong Kong office with many Chinese customers, some of whom were on this list. However, the insurance we provided was not considered the purchase of public securities, so we could offer the insurance.

Whether you want to provide this insurance is another matter. The insurance company's reputational risk is a fair consideration when deciding to provide any services, even allowed transactions, to someone on one of OFAC's watchlists.

Guidance and Frequently Asked Questions (FAQs)

If you're still uncertain whether you can provide insurance, pay claims, or conduct a specific transaction, two additional sources to review that may assist you in deciding if your transaction is allowed are guidance and FAQs.

OFAC sometimes issues guidance on topics like complying with humanitarian general licenses and providing legal help to sanctioned parties. They have also issued over one thousand FAQs that answer common questions about their rules. These FAQs cover everything from what OFAC does to specifics about what you can and can't do under different sanctions programs or with newly sanctioned parties.

But remember, guidance and FAQs are not the same as licenses or regulations; they don't have the force of law. Instead, they are more like this guide, helping you understand and comply with sanctions. Interpretations can and do change over time, so staying updated and consulting with internal or external legal counsel when needed is essential.

11

Insurance Matters Complicating Sanctions Compliance

Insurance companies face various sanctions-related challenges in policy administration. Below, I outline some common issues and provide tips on effectively addressing these risks.

Third-Party Claimants

One of the tougher sanctions challenges is dealing with claimants who aren't customers of the insurance company. This often arises with third-party auto claims, where a non-customer files a claim under the customer's insurance policy. In these cases, you usually have very little information about the claimant—just a name and an address, which is often the attorney's office. If your screening system flags a potential match, it can be hard to get more details, especially if the claimant's attorney is unwilling to share information.

When this happens, we would temporarily hold the payment and ask the claims handler to try to get the needed information, like a date of birth, from the customer or their attorney. We'd let them know we couldn't process the payment until we received the information. Since people wanted their money, we usually got the details we needed.

Multiple Insureds

Corporate policies can cover a wide range of parties, including branch locations, subsidiaries, owners, executives, officers, directors, employees, and even third parties, like in a construction contract or bond. This information is usually found in the application and policy documents but often doesn't get into the screening system unless someone manually scans it. To address this:

- Have the underwriter manually scan all parties to a policy.
- Work with your information technology team to create an automated process that captures all parties in the administrative system and pulls those names into a data file for your sanctions screening solution.
- Refer higher-risk policies (like those in high-risk jurisdictions) to sanctions compliance for review and scanning of all parties, as discussed in a prior chapter.

In my previous job, we used a combination of all three options, depending on whether the system could capture all parties and the potential sanctions risk of the policy.

Claims Issues

Some prohibited transactions may still slip through even with strong sanctions clauses or exclusion language in your policies. For example, you might insure a boat for hull damage, and the owner leases it to another company that takes it to Cuba, where it breaks down. Or you could insure a shipment that sinks in Crimean waters and needs local vendors to salvage it.

You can't pay a claim that would violate sanctions, but you might not be able to deny or block it either. Lloyd's recently introduced a new sanctions clause (LMA3200), which allows for suspending coverage or payment until the potential sanctions violation no longer exists. This language is becoming popular among customers. Depending on the contract terms, the claim might have to remain unresolved for years, in case sanctions change and it becomes legal to pay it. Alternatively, you or the customer can apply for a specific license from OFAC to settle the claim.

Reinsurance

Reinsurance brings its own challenges when it comes to sanctions compliance. As a reinsurer, you're responsible for ensuring that the policies and claims you cover aren't violating sanctions, even if you don't always get the full details from the primary insurance company. Typically, you might receive a summary of premiums or claims (known as a bordereau), which may not include the names of the policyholders or claimants.

Reinsurers should request the names of policyholders and claimants, scan them, and ensure you're not providing coverage to a sanctioned party. It's possible that a policy could be legal for the primary insurance company to insure but not for you to reinsure, depending on jurisdiction. For example, a foreign insurance company may legally provide coverage to an Iranian or Cuban firm, but this could be a sanctions violation for you.

You can't rely on the primary insurance company or broker to perform the scans correctly. In one case, we found that a customer we were reinsuring was sanctioned, which was missed by the broker because they only scanned customers in sanctioned countries. This customer was in a non-sanctioned country but was owned by an Iranian entity. Always perform the scans yourself.

Start by focusing on higher-risk portfolios, like reinsurance involving clients in the Middle East or Russia, or portfolios that cover high-risk products like credit and political risk. Begin by obtaining and scanning the names of policyholders and claimants in those reinsurance contracts before moving on to less risky areas, like property coverage in European countries.

If you're unsure whether OFAC targets reinsurers, look at the case of Gen Re, which was fined by OFAC for paying two reinsurance claims to the Steamship Mutual Underwriting Association Limited for losses from the National Iranian Tanker Company, an SDN.[49]

Third-Party Business Partners

Insurance providers typically outsource a number of activities. You might outsource underwriting (to a Managing General Agent), claims handling (to a third-party administrator for life insurance policies), or information technology. Or your company could contract with a consultant to generate business. These arrangements can open you up to inadvertent sanctions violations as third parties can act independently of your sanctions requirements.

It is important to conduct thorough due diligence on your vendors to identify higher-risk business partners up front (for ongoing monitoring) and to train them on your expectations regarding sanctions.

As part of your vendor contracting process, request the following information to vet for any sanctions issues:

- name and location of the company
- ownership of the company
- ultimate beneficial owners of the company (if different from ownership)
- if any executives or board members are on any sanctions watchlists
- what countries they will be working on your company's contract in
- any sanctions-related fines or judgments in the last five years

In addition to reviewing the vendor's answers to these questions, you should conduct a negative news search for any sanctions-related issues in the last five years.

Realize that some companies will use subsidiaries or branches in other countries to perform the contract work. You need to identify those countries to verify that they do not have trade embargoes or other sanctions issues.

But don't stop vendor management after the contracting phase. If the contract with the vendor lasts for several years, you should perform ongoing monitoring. The frequency will depend on the vendor's risk. Less frequent monitoring can be done on more minor contracts with US companies. More frequent reviews (such as annually) should be conducted for large contracts with companies performing key activities (such as processing payments) overseas.

You should also train your third-party contractors, but that doesn't necessarily mean you have to provide a training course to them. Your organization may have a vendor code of ethics, where you can detail your expectations regarding sanctions compliance. Or, you may have specific procedures for conducting your business that the vendor must follow, including requirements for OFAC scanning.

One insurance company was fined by OFAC due to the actions (or inaction) of their third-party administrator (TPA).[50] The TPA managed the health insurance policies for the insurer, but neither the TPA nor the insurer scanned the names of two customers who were later added to the SDN list.

Your contract with any vendor should clearly state who is responsible for OFAC scanning. If the third party handles it, your organization must oversee its process to ensure the scans are performed correctly.

Sanctions Clause Not Allowed

In this guide, I've stressed the importance of including sanctions exclusion clauses in policies and contracts to protect your company from violations and lawsuits. However, some countries, like Israel and, to a certain extent, Japan, do not allow these clauses in their policies. If you're writing a policy in these countries, you may be unable to add a sanctions exclusion clause.

OFAC addresses this issue in FAQ #103[51] and recommends applying for a specific OFAC license to provide coverage and a separate license to pay claims. However, this process can be time-consuming and complex. It's best to work with legal counsel to develop alternative protective language that complies with the country's restrictions on sanctions clauses.

Trade Sanctions Administered by Other Governmental Agencies

US trade sanctions are managed by different agencies, such as the Department of State (DoS) and the Bureau of Industry and Security (BIS) under the Department of Commerce. Depending on the insurance products you provide, you may need to be familiar with the sanctions enforced by these agencies.

Each agency has its own list of "SDNs" prohibited from exporting goods requiring a license because they previously exported without the proper license. These goods are usually related to arms, defense, or military purposes. You will also need to check your customers against these watchlists to verify you are not covering a prohibited transaction.

In some cases, these entities can still sell goods within the US and Canada, which can be insured. Exports can also be covered if the goods don't require an export license. However, monitoring this can be challenging. For example, we had a customer on the DoS debarred list who continued operations. We had to establish a system that referred each claim made under their policies to the sanctions compliance team to ensure it did not involve exported goods requiring a DoS license.

Additionally, these agencies have lists of US-origin goods that cannot be exported to Russia due to their potential defense or military use. You must check these lists if you are insuring goods bound for Russia.

One company was fined by both BIS and OFAC for exporting pharmaceutical products to Iran without a license.[52]

Ultimate Beneficial Ownership (UBO)

Various legal entities like LLCs, LPs, LLPs, and PLCs are commonly used by sanctioned parties to conceal their assets. These entities often obscure ownership details, especially when incorporated in jurisdictions like Jersey or the Cayman Islands with opaque registration rules. Sanctioned individuals may further complicate matters by structuring these entities to be owned by other entities, making uncovering true ownership challenging. If you provide commercial insurance or inland marine insurance (which covers things like artwork), your book of business likely contains these types of entities.

Some companies, such as Dow Jones and Lexis Nexis, have compiled databases of the ultimate beneficial owner of various legal entities. In addition, these entities must file beneficial ownership information with FinCEN under the Beneficial Ownership Information Reporting Rule.[53]

However, these databases aren't infallible. When dealing with customers operating under one of these legal entities, requesting information and documentation of ultimate beneficial ownership is essential to ensure compliance and avoid engaging with sanctioned parties. Russian oligarchs, in particular, use these vehicles to hide assets, ownership, and control of their businesses.

UBOs can create challenges for insurance companies. Recently, OFAC fined PURE Insurance for this issue.[54] Their corporate customer was wholly owned by a person who was added to the SDN list. However, PURE's scanning system only tracked the corporate customer's name, not the UBO's. As a result, the account wasn't flagged or blocked, leading to an OFAC fine.

This example shows why it's essential for insurance companies to not only track corporate clients but also identify and scan for any sanctioned UBOs to avoid compliance violations.

Mergers and Acquisitions (M&A)

Insurance companies frequently buy another insurance company or a specific book of business. Sanctions compliance should always be involved in M&A discussions as they will need to assist in vetting the company for any sanctions issues. You don't want to buy a company that later gets you an OFAC fine, such as the Ace/Chubb merger.[55]

The challenges of incorporating a purchased insurance entity into your organization are too numerous to discuss in this guide. However, start with vetting the company to determine if there are or were any sanctions penalties against them, how those issues were resolved, any open investigations, what their book of business consists of (products and jurisdictions), and establishing some initial oversight over those higher risk areas.

Reputational Risk

The risk to your organization's reputation from a sanctions violation might not come up often, but it's a genuine concern. Today, customers and business partners, like banks, consider more than just price—they also care about a company's ethics and reputation. Negative publicity from a sanctions issue can hurt your company's bottom line even more than an OFAC penalty.

For example, a few years ago, the US government considered naming companies, including insurance firms, involved in business related to the Nord Stream 2 pipeline, which carries natural gas from Russia and is a major revenue source for them. The US wanted work on this pipeline to cease. Eventually, they did release some names of companies that had stopped their involvement with the pipeline, including two large insurers. Although these actions weren't necessarily sanctions violations at the time for these companies, it raises the question: would you want your company named on such a list?

When reviewing policies and claims with potential sanctions issues or other negative news, bring findings to management's attention so they are fully informed before taking on a risk.

Specific Issues by Insurance Product

Consumer Insurance

Consumer insurance is generally considered a lower-risk product since you can usually obtain and scan all policyholders for sanctions. However, some risk still exists, so you can't skip basic sanctions procedures like scanning in this business line. Even minor violations can lead to actions from OFAC.

For example, Geico received a small fine from OFAC for providing auto insurance to a person on the SDN list. [56] While the fine was minor, the reputational damage can be more significant.

Group Employee Benefits

Your group benefits policyholder might be a company, but the claimant and underlying insureds or beneficiaries are often individuals. Should you scan all these people upfront, and what if those covered individuals change? OFAC doesn't require scanning all beneficiaries of a group policy unless you receive a list of those individuals. If you do, OFAC expects you to screen them.

OFAC has stated that if an insurer knows a person covered under a group policy is on the SDN list (which you would see if you received a list of covered employees), that person's coverage is blocked. If they file a claim, the insurer cannot pay it. If you don't know the names of the people covered under a group policy, you wouldn't need to block anything until an SDN files a claim, at which point the blocking requirement would apply. [57]

So, if you don't currently receive lists of all individuals covered under a group contract, OFAC does not require you to do so. You should implement procedures to vet those individuals at claim time.

Beneficiaries of life insurance and accidental death and dismemberment policies can be located anywhere in the world, including in sanctioned jurisdictions. As I previously described, finding a legal way to pay out some of these valid claims is difficult.

Ransomware

It's best (for you!) if your organization doesn't provide coverage for ransomware attacks, as they come with significant sanctions risks and often involve limited information about the breach or the bad actors involved. OFAC discourages paying ransoms because they usually benefit sanctioned individuals or groups, including those associated with sanctioned jurisdictions.

Ransomware attacks can involve various sanctioned entities, such as individuals, organizations (which may disband and reorganize under a new name), specific ransomware versions, or even the crypto wallet addresses used for payment. In smaller ransom cases, your customer might just pay the ransom without hiring an incident response firm like Coveware. These firms specialize in identifying attackers, assessing the attack method, and performing initial sanctions reviews with tools that most insurance companies don't have. These firms can sometimes trace payments to their destinations, adding another layer of security.

If an incident response firm is involved, review its report to confirm what sanctions screening was conducted and its results. We did have one or two occasions where the firm recommended not paying the ransom and did not assist the customer in paying the ransom due to a sanctions issue. If the incident response firm recommends not paying a ransom, your organization certainly should not.

If no firm is involved, your organization will need to conduct these scans, even though your customer may have little knowledge of the ransomware software used or the hacking group involved. Emails or screenshots of ransom demands may provide clues, which you can research online to identify the group behind them.

A growing trend in the insurance industry is for the insurer to pay the ransom directly through a cryptocurrency operator rather than reimburse the customer. Regardless of the payment method, it still raises sanctions concerns as the insurance company will pay the ransom directly to the offender or indirectly through the customer.

Do your best to conduct thorough due diligence now and document every step taken. Even if a sanctions issue is discovered later, having detailed records of your due diligence efforts will be crucial for defending your actions with OFAC.

Travel Insurance

As previously mentioned, global travel insurance coverage is usually allowed, but exceptions exist. Cuban travel seems to trip up insurers the most. Travel to Cuba must be under one of the authorized general licenses before an insurance company can provide coverage.

When we provided travel insurance for school groups going to Cuba, we had to conduct thorough checks to ensure compliance with these licenses by:

1. Reviewing the detailed daily agenda to ensure it meets the general license terms. We denied coverage for trips with too much touristy sightseeing time.
2. Obtaining a signed affidavit from the travel provider confirming that the trip met the terms of the general license (usually support for the Cuban people or educational).
3. Collecting and keeping the names of all travelers going to Cuba.

If you don't follow these rules when providing travel insurance for trips to Cuba, you risk facing OFAC fines. For example, one US insurance company was fined by OFAC because their Canadian branch, considered a US person by OFAC, issued travel insurance policies that occasionally covered Canadian residents traveling to Cuba.[58]

Ocean Marine

Marine insurance is one of the higher-risk areas when it comes to sanctions, mainly because of all the moving parts involved. There are many parties to keep track of, including the shipper, receiver, consignee, freight forwarder, ultimate beneficiary, the ship (including its owner and crew company), agents, goods (oil —be careful complying with the Russia oil price cap sanctions), and shipment routes (is the route going through a sanctioned jurisdiction?). Whether you're insuring the ship itself or the goods being transported, each party needs to be identified and checked against sanctions lists. Some insurers even check the names of the ship's crew.

The situation is further complicated by the fact that some shipping firms are skilled at evading detection. They might briefly turn off their AIS (Automated Identification System) tracker to move goods to banned locations like Russia or

North Korea. Alternatively, oil tankers may transfer oil at sea from one ship to another to avoid detection, with the final destination being a sanctioned country.

Having a strong sanctions exclusion clause in your policy is crucial to managing these risks. Detailed due diligence on claims is also essential. This might include checking the certificate of origin for goods or reviewing the ship's route to ensure it didn't pass through any prohibited areas or experience periods when the AIS was turned off.

One insurance company was fined by OFAC because it insured shipments transhipping or destined for a sanctioned country.[59]

Credit and Political Risk

These types of policies typically are higher risk for sanctions as well. Credit risk may have counterparties that may not be known until claim time. There could also be claimants in sanctioned jurisdictions, or part of the transaction has a nexus to a sanctioned country.

We had a foreign financial institution customer with a credit risk policy. The institution held a portfolio of bonds. The financial institution was sued for not properly managing the bonds, resulting in losses to the investors. It came to us for payment under the policy. Unfortunately, two of the bonds in the portfolio were Cuban government bonds, and we were advised we couldn't pay the claim.

In a second instance, a company filed a claim under the credit risk policy when their customer defaulted on a loan. Unfortunately, their customer had recently been sanctioned, which led to the default, and we were not able to pay the claim since it involved an SDN.

12

Managing US Parent Versus Foreign Branch or Subsidiary Conflicts

Global insurance companies sometimes face disagreements between their US headquarters and foreign branches or subsidiaries about whether to take on particular business. The US parent company might be cautious about approving business that's legal for the foreign office but could lead to future sanctions or reputational problems. On the other hand, the foreign office might want to pursue business even if the US parent company believes it could violate sanctions. Resolving these conflicts can be challenging due to legal and regulatory barriers and can lead to tension between legal/compliance and business units, especially when the business comes from VIP brokers or offers high premiums. Executives in the line of business may push back against compliance advice not to write these policies.

So, can these conflicts be resolved or at least managed?

Ultimately, the line of business can choose to write whatever they want; your role is to educate them about the sanctions risks and potential violations involved. If they proceed with writing prohibited business, you will need to decide whether to self-report the violation, which can reduce a future OFAC penalty. They might also choose to write business that you know, based on your deep understanding of current sanctions, will eventually be prohibited—creating more work to unwind later.

Many companies have been fined by OFAC for violations their foreign subsidiaries or branches incurred, some of which conducted the transaction after the US parent company told them to cease that activity. One example is Black and Decker, which was fined by OFAC because its Chinese subsidiary exported or tried to export tools to Iran.[60]

The following are two potential solutions we utilized to manage these conflicts.

Risk Decision Matrix

Documenting the decision-making process in a risk decision matrix could be valuable. It shows who in the company is responsible for decisions on sanctions-related issues. My prior organization had one, and we often referred to it during challenging discussions about policies or claims with a sanctions nexus. Our matrix was simply an Excel spreadsheet with five levels of decision-making depending on the situation.

Tier 1: Business line staff make the decisions. No sanctions issue exists, so the employees conduct business as usual.

Tier 2: The sanctions compliance team makes the decision. Someone on the sanctions team can resolve a potential sanctions issue, such as clearing a false positive match.

Tier 3: The SCO or the sanctions compliance team manager decides. Potential business that may violate sanctions is escalated to the manager or SCO. They can decline the business if a transaction or account violates sanctions. Otherwise, if necessary, they can resolve the issue with input from other company staff.

Tier 4: Business line management makes the decision. Usually, these decisions are risk-related. The customer or transaction is at high risk for a potential sanctions violation, so the decision is whether to accept the customer or conduct the transaction. Business line management has the final say, although the SCO and legal counsel may provide their input during decision-making. This tier is not for transactions that clearly violate sanctions; that decision rests in Tier 3 with sanctions compliance staff.

Tier 5: Senior management participates in the decision. A sanctions violation may have occurred, so executive management determines the response (such as self-reporting to OFAC) with input from the SCO, legal counsel, and business line staff.

Recusal Policy

Another way to manage these conflicts is by implementing an internal recusal policy. If your foreign subsidiary is legally allowed to write business that your US entity cannot, the transaction may be able to proceed as long as all US involvement is avoided, including any participation from US staff.

For example, your subsidiary has an opportunity to write a policy that involves the Venezuelan government, an OFAC-sanctioned group. If there is no other US nexus (no US parties involved in the policy, it's not denominated in US dollars, and transactions don't include US financial institutions, for example), then the business may be allowable if a recusal policy is followed.

We established a recusal policy where US employees, such as underwriters, claims adjusters, and managers, were excluded from participating in specific policies and claims throughout their duration. The potential business was referred to the sanctions compliance team for review, which informed the foreign subsidiary that US employees couldn't participate in that policy or claim.

However, this won't work in situations involving Iran or Cuba since foreign subsidiaries are US persons under those regulations.

One exception to recusal is that US employees can still offer legal and compliance advice to their foreign counterparts on complying with US sanctions and whether a transaction is prohibited by OFAC.[61]

If you institute a recusal policy, be careful that no US person gets involved in handling or decision-making on the activity. One company was fined by OFAC because US senior managers approved contracts for a foreign subsidiary, violating Directive 4 of the Ukraine-/Russia-related Sanctions.[62] This fine may not have occurred if a recusal policy had been properly followed.

13
Penalties for Non-Compliance

OFAC is responsible for civil enforcement of US sanctions laws and regulations. Violations can result in substantial fines, and civil and criminal penalties can exceed several million dollars.[63] Other governmental agencies, such as the Department of Justice (DOJ) or the New York Department of Financial Services, can also impose their own penalties for the same conduct. Throughout this guide, I've noted several instances where insurance companies have been penalized by OFAC. Below are a couple larger fines that illustrate the extent to which a company may be subject to penalties.

British American Tobacco (BAT) settled with OFAC for $508 million for violations of the weapons proliferation and North Korea sanctions regulations. BAT is UK-based, and its foreign subsidiary in Singapore was also involved in these transactions, so they aren't automatically US persons for purposes of these regulations. However, the transactions had a US nexus, specifically using a US correspondent banking account and a foreign branch of a US bank to clear these transactions.[64]

The largest fine to date happened in November 2023, totaling $968 million, against Binance. Government agencies such as the Financial Crimes Enforcement Network (FinCEN), Internal Revenue Service (IRS), and DOJ were also involved. Binance got in trouble for not setting up systems to spot and report suspicious transactions involving terrorists, ransomware gangs, money launderers, and other criminals. OFAC said Binance purposely undermined and ineffectually implemented its own sanctions compliance controls.[65]

Besides fines, employees, officers, and directors face severe consequences like losing their jobs or going to jail. The DOJ and the US Attorney might bring criminal charges. For instance, in 2022, a US citizen was sentenced to more than five years in prison. He violated IEEPA by helping North Korea use blockchain and cryptocurrency to hide money and avoid US sanctions.[66]

It is important to note that OFAC operates on a strict liability basis. This means you can be fined for a violation of any amount (in theory, one dollar), even if you did not intend to violate sanctions. However, penalties will depend, in part, on the amount of the violation, whether it was inadvertent or deliberate, and whether you identified and reported the breach to OFAC.

And again, don't overlook the damage to your reputation and your company's reputation when OFAC releases a press statement about your violation. Bad publicity and all the negative fallout from that violation can hurt your finances even more. Banks and customers might use this negative news to decide whether to work with you.

14
Conclusion

Staying informed about economic sanctions is essential for insurance companies and their employees. These sanctions, enforced by OFAC, can seriously impact your organization, and failing to comply may lead to costly penalties and damage your company's reputation in the marketplace.

Sanctions are constantly changing, and staying up-to-date is key. New programs and watchlists are implemented or revised regularly and what's allowed today may not be tomorrow. With the knowledge gained from this guide, alongside other available resources, you can keep up with these shifts and ensure your business remains compliant. By being proactive, you can navigate the complex sanctions landscape with confidence.

Remember, compliance isn't just about avoiding fines but about upholding ethical and legal standards in a complex global landscape. By following sanctions regulations, insurers and their employees help promote international stability and security and foster trust in the insurance industry.

15

Test Your Knowledge

Now, it is time to test your knowledge of the concepts presented in this guide.

Questions

1. You work for a US-based insurer that wants to sign a contract to sell products to the Government of Venezuela. Can you do this business?
   a. Would your answer change if you worked for the foreign branch of the US-based company?
   b. Would your answer change if you worked for the foreign subsidiary of the US-based company?

2. You work for a US-based insurance company, and your US customer filed a claim to be reimbursed for the repair of her Persian rug. She sent her rug to Iran for repair. Can you pay this claim?
   a. Yes. Our customer is a US person and has not been sanctioned.
   b. No.

3. Your customer wants to do business with A Russian Company, an entity on the Sectoral Sanctions Identifications list. Can you insure this business?
   a. No, they are sanctioned, so we can't insure the business.
   b. Possibly, depending on the business they want to do with them.
   c. Yes, the sectoral sanctions list is a non-SDN sanctions list, so we can insure the business.

4. You have a new business consultant, Jose Morales, in Texas. Do you need to scan this person through the OFAC lists?
   a. Yes. You have to scan all business partners.
   b. No. He's a US person, so he wouldn't be sanctioned.

5. Your insurance company is asked to provide townhome insurance to Oligarch Property Management, LLC. The management company is listed as the owner of the property. You scan the management company, and it is not sanctioned. However, you learn by talking to one of the employees that the beneficial owner of the property is a Russian person. When you scan the name, you find out he is sanctioned. Can you provide this insurance?

a. No. A sanctioned party is the beneficial owner of the property.

b. Yes. Our customer is the management company, which isn't sanctioned.

6. You want to provide insurance to XYZ Company in the UK. You know XYZ Company is a subsidiary of a Russian energy company. You scan XYZ Company, and they are not on the SDN list. Are you clear to do business with them?

a. No

b. Yes

c. Not yet

7. A Canadian firm with a branch in Russia wants your US-based insurance company to provide liability insurance to its entire organization. The Russian branch is sanctioned by OFAC. Are any of the following responses appropriate?

a. You can't issue the policy through your US writing company, but refer it to your UK subsidiary to write.

b. You can write the policy if there is a territorial exclusion for Russia and the Russian branch.

c. You can't issue the policy because one of the branches is sanctioned, which means the entire organization is sanctioned.

8. You provide group life insurance to a corporate customer. They provide you with a list of all employees. Do you have to scan this list to ensure no employees are SDNs?

a. No. The corporation is our customer.

b. Yes. OFAC expects that if you have the names, you scan them.

9. You provide Directors and Officers insurance to a global company. There is a claim under the policy for a director. When you scan the director's name, you find they were recently sanctioned. What do you do?

a. Pay the claim directly to the non-sanctioned global company.

b. Deny the claim.

c. Block the claim payment.

10. Your company provides Ocean Marine insurance to cover the shipment of medical supplies to India. You scan all parties involved in the shipment and discover the vessel is sanctioned. Can you provide the insurance?

a. No. A party to the shipment is sanctioned, so the entire transaction is prohibited.
b. Yes. Our customer is not sanctioned.
c. Yes. It involves medical supplies, which fall under a humanitarian general license.

Answers

1. No. The Government of Venezuela is sanctioned by OFAC.

   a. No. Foreign branches are US persons subject to OFAC regulations for all sanctions programs.

   b. Maybe. The foreign subsidiary may be able to do this business as it is not subject to OFAC regulations. However, verify there is no US nexus to the insurance and implement a recusal policy.

2. B. You cannot reimburse your customer for this expense. The customer had the rug repaired in Iran and paid an Iranian company for the work. As a commercial entity, your insurance company would indirectly provide funds to the Iranian company by reimbursing the claim, which OFAC prohibits.

3. B. Depending on the business the customer wants to do with them, you may be able to conduct it. If your customer wants to sell A Russian Company computer parts, it's likely to be a prohibited transaction that you cannot insure. If, instead, your customer wants to import grain from Russia, that is likely an allowable transaction.

4. A. You have to scan anyone you do business with through OFAC, no matter where they are located, as anyone anywhere in the world, including the US, can be on the SDN list.

5. A. The beneficial owner of the townhome you are asked to insure is sanctioned. The townhome is "frozen" by its sanctioned ownership, and you can't provide services, such as insurance, for it.

6. C. Knowing they are owned by a Russian company and that it operates in an industry that has been subject to sanctions, you should also scan the Russian owner through OFAC. If they are sanctioned and own more than 50 percent of XYZ Company, then XYZ Company is deemed sanctioned, and you either can't do any business with them or can't do certain transactions with them.

7. B is the best response. As long as that sanctioned branch is excluded from coverage via a territorial exclusion, you should be able to insure the rest of the company. Referring a firm to your subsidiary that may be able to provide a service you cannot due to OFAC sanctions could be considered facilitation (choice A), and the entire company is not sanctioned just by virtue of a branch being sanctioned (choice C).

8. B. Yes, OFAC expects that you would have scanned the names if you have them. However, if the company did not provide you with the roster of covered employees, you do not have to request and scan them.

9. C. You cannot pay a claim involving a sanctioned party, even if the insured is not sanctioned. However, you also cannot deny the claim if it's valid. In this case, you may need to reject the transaction if the funds are considered the property of the company rather than the sanctioned individual. If the funds belong to the sanctioned director, you must block the payment (if the claim was processed before they became an SDN), apply for an OFAC license to pay the claim, or let the claim remain unresolved until sanctions change, allowing you to complete the process.

10. A. A party to the transaction (in this case, the vessel) is sanctioned, so the entire transaction is prohibited. Just because your customer is not sanctioned doesn't mean the transaction is legal. A humanitarian general license is not applicable as India, the ultimate destination, is not a sanctioned jurisdiction and has no general licenses available.

References

Below is a good reference list of websites with further details on the information provided in this guide.

All OFAC Sanctions Programs

https://ofac.treasury.gov/sanctions-programs-and-country-information

OFAC Frequently Asked Questions

https://ofac.treasury.gov/faqs/all-faqs

Free OFAC List Search Tool

https://sanctionssearch.ofac.treas.gov/

OFAC Compliance Guidance for Sanctions Programs

https://ofac.treasury.gov/media/16331/download?inline

UK Sanctions Programs

https://www.gov.uk/government/collections/financial-sanctions-regime-specific-consolidated-lists-and-releases

EU Sanctions Programs

https://www.sanctionsmap.eu/#/main

OFAC Enforcement Actions

https://ofac.treasury.gov/civil-penalties-and-enforcement-information

Author Biography

Heidi Hunter worked for a US-based insurance company with global operations for over a decade. She developed and managed the company's sanctions compliance program, covering all its locations. She oversaw the team responsible for complying with sanctions and worked closely with other teams within the company to ensure they understood and followed sanctions regulations. Heidi has a Master of Business Administration (MBA) and is a Certified Public Accountant (inactive).

Visit her website at https://easysanctions.wordpress.com/ for more information on sanctions and to sign up for her newsletter.

All Books in the Plain-English Guide Series by Heidi Hunter

The Plain-English Guide to Economic Sanctions

The Plain-English Guide to Developing an Economic Sanctions Program

The Plain-English Guide to Economic Sanctions Risk Assessments

The Plain-English Guide to Economic Sanctions for Insurance Companies

The Plain-English Guide to Economic Sanctions for Foreign Companies

Companion Workbooks:

The Plain-English Guide to Developing an Economic Sanctions Program Workbook

The Plain-English Guide to Economic Sanctions Risk Assessments Workbook

Find them all at: https://easysanctions.wordpress.com/books/

If you read one of my guides, please post a rating or review!

Notes

1. European Union Sanctions, https://www.eeas.europa.eu/eeas/european-union-sanctions_en.

2. OFAC, Frequently Asked Questions, FAQ 10, https://ofac.treasury.gov/faqs/all-faqs.

3. "Overview of US Sanctions," Wilkie Compliance, accessed April 25, 2024, https://complianceconcourse.willkie.com/resources/sanctions-us-overview-of-us-sanctions/.

4. Edward J. Collins-Chase, "Sanctions Primer: How the United States Uses Restrictive Mechanisms to Advance Foreign Policy or National Security Objectives" (Congressional Research Service, 2023), https://crsreports.congress.gov/product/pdf/R/R47829.

5. OFAC, Other OFAC Sanctions Lists, https://ofac.treasury.gov/other-ofac-sanctions-lists; OFAC, FAQ 91.

6. OFAC, Ukraine-/Russia-related Sanctions, https://ofac.treasury.gov/sanctions-programs-and-country-information/ukraine-russia-related-sanctions.

7. OFAC, Other Lists, Non-SDN Menu Based Sanctions List, https://ofac.treasury.gov/other-ofac-sanctions-lists.

8. OFAC, "Determination Pursuant to Section 1(a)(i) of Executive Order 14024," May 8, 2022, https://ofac.treasury.gov/media/922951/download?inline; OFAC, FAQ 1061.

9. OFAC, FAQ 1061.

10. Executive Order 14068, "Prohibiting Certain Imports, Exports, and New Investment with Respect to Continued Russian Federation Aggression," March 11, 2022, https://ofac.treasury.gov/media/919281/download?inline.

11. Executive Order 14066 "Prohibiting Certain Imports and New Investments with Respect to Continued Russian Federation Efforts To Undermine the Sovereignty and Territorial Integrity of Ukraine," March 8, 2022, https://ofac.treasury.gov/media/919111/download?inline.

12. OFAC, Determination Pursuant to Section 1(a)(i)(A) of Executive Order 14068, "Prohibitions Related to Imports of Aluminum, Copper, and Nickel of Russian Federation Origin," https://ofac.treasury.gov/media/932796/download?inline.

13. Bureau of Industry and Security, Common High Priority List, https://www.bis.gov/articles/russia-export-controls-list-common-high-priority-items.

14. OFAC, FAQ 91.

15. Executive Order 13884, "Blocking Property of the Government of Venezuela," August 5, 2019, https://ofac.treasury.gov/media/26786/download?inline.

16. OFAC, FAQ 91.

17. Department of the Treasury, "Revised Guidance on Entities Owned by Persons Whose Property and Interests in Property Are Blocked," https://ofac.treasury.gov/media/6186/download?inline; OFAC, FAQ 399.

18. OFAC, FAQ 11.

19. "What are Secondary Sanctions?" Dow Jones Risk & Compliance Glossary, accessed April 25, 2024, https://www.dowjones.com/professional/risk/glossary/sanctions/secondary-sanctions/.

20. Executive Order 14114, "Taking Additional Steps with Respect to the Russian Federation's Harmful Activities," December 22, 2023, https://ofac.treasury.gov/media/932441/download?inline.

21. *Code of Federal Regulations*, Cuban Asset Control Regulations, 31 CFR§ 515.329, https://www.ecfr.gov/current/title-31/subtitle-B/chapter-V/part-515?toc=1.

22. *Code of Federal Regulations*, Iranian Transactions and Sanctions Regulations, 31 CFR§ 560.215, https://www.ecfr.gov/current/title-31/subtitle-B/chapter-V/part-560?toc=1.

23. EU Council Regulation (E.C.) No 2271/96 of November 22, 1996, as amended by Commission Delegated Regulation (E.U.) 2018/1100 of June 6, 2018, https://www.legislation.gov.uk/eur/1996/2271; "Spotlight on the U.K. Protection of Trading Interests Legislation," Wilkie Compliance, accessed April 25, 2024, https://complianceconcourse.willkie.com/resources/sanctions-uk-uk-blocking-statute/.

24. HM Treasury, Office of Financial Sanctions Implementation, "Ownership and Control: Public Officials and Control Guidance," accessed April 25, 2024, https://www.gov.uk/government/publications/ownership-and-control-public-officials-and-control-guidance/ownership-and-control-public-officials-and-control-guidance; Council of the European Union "Restrictive measures (Sanctions) - Update of the EU Best Practices for the Effective Implementation

of Restrictive Measures," May 4, 2018, Section VIII Ownership and Control, 22, https://data.consilium.europa.eu/doc/document/ST-8519-2018-INIT/en/pdf.

25. OFAC, FAQ 776.

26. *Code of Federal Regulations*, Iraq Stabilization and Insurgency Sanctions Regulations, § 576.315, https://www.ecfr.gov/current/title-31/subtitle-B/chapter-V/part-576/subpart-C/section-576.315.

27. *Code of Federal Regulations*, § 560.208, Iranian Transactions and Sanctions Regulations, Prohibited Facilitation by United States Persons of Transactions by Foreign Persons, https://www.ecfr.gov/current/title-31/subtitle-B/chapter-V/part-560/subpart-B/section-560.208.

28. OFAC, "Alfa Laval Inc. Settles Potential Civil Liability for Apparent Violations of the Iranian Transactions and Sanctions Regulations," July 19, 2021, https://ofac.treasury.gov/media/911516/download?inline.

29. Department of the Treasury, "A Framework for OFAC Compliance Commitments," https://ofac.treasury.gov/media/16331/download?inline.

30. OFAC, FAQ 102.

31. Lloyds Market Association Bulletin LMA23-028-AR, "Sanctions Clauses," October 5, 2023, https://www.lmalloyds.com/LMA_Bulletins/LMA23-028-AR.aspx.

32. EU Council Regulation (E.C.) No 2271/96 of November 22, 1996, as amended by Commission Delegated Regulation (E.U.) 2018/1100 of June 6, 2018, https://www.legislation.gov.uk/eur/1996/2271; "Spotlight on the U.K. Protection of Trading Interests Legislation," Wilkie Compliance, accessed April 25, 2024, https://complianceconcourse.willkie.com/resources/sanctions-uk-uk-blocking-statute/.

33. Debevoise and Plimpton, "UK High Court Rules on Sanctions Clauses in Insurance Contracts and Considers Application of the EU Blocking Regulation," October 30, 2018, https://www.debevoise.com/-/media/files/insights/publications/-2018/10/20181030_uk_high_court_rules_on_sanctions_clauses_in_insurance_co ntracts_and_considers_application_of_the_eu_blocking_regulation.pdf.

34. Debevoise and Plimpton, "UK High Court Rules on Sanctions Clauses in Insurance Contracts and Considers Application of the EU Blocking Regulation," October 30, 2018, https://www.debevoise.com/media/files/insights/publications/-2018/10/20181030_uk_high_court_rules_on_sanctions_clauses_in_insurance _contracts_and_considers_application_of_the_eu_blocking_regulation.pdf?rev=0

af7e2c9c9fb446dac22ca003c556f33&hash=3F5071D480591373DE20DD68E72 E07CB.

35. Baker McKenzie, "Sanctions clauses and US extraterritorial sanctions – Lamesa v Cynergy appeal," July 10, 2020, https://sanctionsnews.bakermckenzie.com/sanctions-clauses-and-us-extraterritorial-sanctions-lamesa-v-cynergy-appeal/.

36. Wilmer Hale, "Top EU Court Rules on the EU Blocking Regulation Against US Sanctions for the First Time," January 31, 2022, https://www.wilmerhale.com/insights/client-alerts/20220124-top-eu-court-rules-on-the-eu-blocking-regulation-against-us-sanctions-for-the-first-time.

37. OFAC Sanctions List Search, https://sanctionssearch.ofac.treas.gov/.

38. Department of the Treasury, "OFAC Issues a Finding of Violation to MidFirst Bank for Violations of the Weapons of Mass Destruction Proliferators Sanctions Regulations," July 21, 2022, https://ofac.treasury.gov/media/924506/download?inline.

39. OFAC, FAQ 9.

40. OFAC, FAQ 63.

41. OFAC, FAQ 9.

42. OFAC, FAQ 49.

43. OFAC, FAQ 8.

44. OFAC, "Supplemental Guidance for The Provision of Humanitarian Assistance," February 27, 2023, https://ofac.treasury.gov/media/931341/download?inline; FAQ 1105.

45. OFAC, "United Medical Instruments Inc. Settles Potential Civil Liability for Alleged Violations of the Iranian Transactions and Sanctions Regulations," February, 28, 2017, https://ofac.treasury.gov/media/11181/download?inline.

46. OFAC, FAQs 227, 243, 453, 462, 732.

47. OFAC, FAQ 74.

48. OFAC, FAQ 905.

49. OFAC, Gen Re Settles Iranian Transactions Regulations Allegations, June 29, 2011, https://ofac.treasury.gov/media/13836/download?inline.

50. OFAC, "AXA Equitable Life Insurance Company Receives a Finding of Violation Regarding Violations of the Foreign Narcotics Kingpin Sanctions

Regulations," August 2, 2016,
https://ofac.treasury.gov/media/11666/download?inline.

51. OFAC, FAQ 103.

52. OFAC, "Alcon Laboratories, Inc., Alcon Pharmaceuticals Ltd., and Alcon Management, SA, Settle Potential Civil Liability for Apparent Violations of the Iranian Transactions and Sanctions Regulations and the Sudanese Sanctions Regulations," July 5, 2016,
https://ofac.treasury.gov/media/11641/download?inline#:~:text=OFAC%20deter mined%20that%20Alcon%20did,the%20Apparent%20Violations%20was%20% 2416%2C927%2C000.

53. FinCEN, Beneficial Ownership Information, Frequently Asked Questions, https://www.fincen.gov/boi-faqs.

54. OFAC, "OFAC Settles with Privilege Underwriters Reciprocal Exchange for $466,200 Related to Apparent Violations of the Ukraine-/Russia-Related Sanctions Regulations," December 21, 2023,
https://ofac.treasury.gov/media/932486/download?inline.

55. OFAC, "Chubb Limited (as Successor Legal Entity of the Former ACE Limited) Settles Potential Liability for Apparent Violations of the Cuban Assets Control Regulations," December 9, 2019,
https://ofac.treasury.gov/media/25921/download?inline.

56. OFAC, "GEICO General Insurance Company Settles Foreign Narcotics Kingpin Sanctions Regulations Allegations," June 3, 2010,
https://ofac.treasury.gov/media/13131/download?inline.

57. OFAC, FAQ 64.

58. OFAC, "Allianz Global Risks US Insurance Company Settles Potential Liability for Apparent Violations of the Cuban Assets Control Regulations," December 19, 2019, https://ofac.treasury.gov/media/25926/download?inline.

59. OFAC, "American International Group, Inc. Settles Potential Liability for Apparent Violations of Multiple Sanctions Programs," June 26, 2017,
https://ofac.treasury.gov/media/11141/download?inline.

60. OFAC, "Stanley Black & Decker, Inc. Settles Potential Civil Liability for Apparent Violations of the Iranian Transactions and Sanctions Regulations Committed by its Chinese-Based Subsidiary Jiangsu Guoqiang Tools Co. Ltd.," March 27, 2019, https://ofac.treasury.gov/media/13911/download?inline.

61. OFAC, "Guidance on the Provision of Certain Services Relating to the Requirements of US Sanctions Laws," January 12, 2017, https://ofac.treasury.gov/media/6211/download?inline.

62. OFAC, "OFAC Settles with Cameron International Corporation for Its Potential Civil Liability for Apparent Violations of Ukraine-Related Sanctions Regulations," September 27, 2021, https://ofac.treasury.gov/media/913321/download?inline.

63. OFAC, FAQ 12.

64. Department of the Treasury, "Treasury Announces $508 Million Settlement with British American Tobacco Largest Ever Against Non-Financial Institution," April 25, 2023, https://home.treasury.gov/news/press-releases/jy1441.

65. Department of the Treasury, Enforcement Release, "OFAC Settles with Binance Holdings, Ltd. for $968,618,825 Related to Apparent Violations of Multiple Sanctions Programs," November 21, 2023, https://ofac.treasury.gov/media/932351/download?inline.

66. Department of Justice, Office of Public Affairs, Press Release, "US Citizen Who Conspired to Assist North Korea in Evading Sanctions Sentenced to Over Five Years and Fined $100,000," April 12, 2022, https://www.justice.gov/opa/pr/us-citizen-who-conspired-assist-north-korea-evading-sanctions-sentenced-over-five-years-and.